BEHIND
THE MASK

JERAMIE MARTIN

CONTENTS

INTRODUCTION

I want to start off by thanking you for reading this book. It truly has been a labor of love. I have a great desire to help others find hope and happiness within.

Growing up I would never have thought that I would be a writer. I still don't see myself as that as much as I do an educator. Going through this process of writing has been one of the most dramatic experiences of my life, and I have had many of those. The internal battles have been quite intense and, at times, even debilitating.

One of my most memorable experiences was when I attended a motivational conference where Les Brown was the keynote speaker. I had listened to his videos on YouTube and just felt such a strong connection with his messages that I really wanted to hear him speak in person. I went to his conference, not realizing I had to first sit through what seemed to be a never-ending barrage of self-improvement sales-pitches from many companies that really just wanted to sell products.

When Les Brown finally came on stage, I felt such a great deal of respect and admiration for him. His messages had meant so much to me in my life at that point. He was just as funny and charismatic in person as he was on his videos, but I could tell he wasn't fully healthy. He had to have assistance to sit in a chair while presenting his speech.

Les started by thanking all of us for being there and for lasting the entire day. Many had left early because of the lengthy conference (and possibly sales pressure), but all that didn't matter to me once he got on stage. Quite a few people remained and felt just as much excitement about seeing him live as I did.

About 15 minutes into his speech, he got serious and, in a softened voice, said, "Now I want to speak to those of you out there who have an internal desire to speak, or write, or feel that you have a message to share with the world." At that very moment I felt as if the whole room went quiet. I felt that he was speaking directly to me—as if he could see me out of everyone there. Les then said,

"Now, you may be wondering why you have this desire, or you may not be sure about what you will speak about, or even if anyone would listen to you. Well, I would like to explain something to you. We are all energetic beings and we are all vibrational beings as well. And what I mean by that is that when you speak, your voice has a specific vibration or frequency to it. Have you ever wondered why you enjoy listening to some individuals so much but not others? Well, that's because you are tuned into their frequency or vibration." Then he said,

"THAT'S THE SAME THING THAT HAPPENS TO US. WHEN WE SPEAK, OUR VIBRATION IS PUT OUT INTO THE WORLD. AND THOSE INDIVIDUALS WHO ARE TUNED INTO <u>OUR</u> FREQUENCY WILL HEAR OUR VIBRATION AND, AS THEY DO THAT, THEY WILL PAY CLOSE ATTENTION TO WHAT YOU ARE SAYING AND THEY WILL COME TO YOU."

"So again, for those of you who have a desire to speak, just know that there are individuals out there who are tuned in and waiting for you to speak. And as you do, they will come to you and benefit from the message you are sharing with them."

As that message from one of the most motivational people I have ever seen settled in, I remember a warm feeling of happiness and joy came over me as I thought about speaking and sharing my story through my voice.

This book is the catalyst for me to share my voice, even in written word, to those who are willing to hear it. Other avenues such as a blog, podcasts, and public speaking events will also be offered.

I want to thank all those who support me and encourage me to pursue this dream. I want to thank those who didn't support me also because they gave me the drive and motivation to keep going.

I want to thank those who spent hours upon hours working with me on this, supporting my efforts with their gifts and talents. I want to thank those who have made it possible for me to create this work, whether directly or indirectly.

I want to thank my kids for always being supportive, even when, at times, they really didn't know or understand what I was doing.

The list can go on and on, but mostly I am thankful that I have the ability to share my story and knowledge. It is my greatest hope that someone out there may find comfort and hope within these pages. It is my greatest desire to help others discover their own greatness and see themselves with as much adoration and admiration as they have when looking at their own heroes.

I firmly believe that we all have a gift to give to the world. Steve Harvey says there are two great works we must perform in this lifetime: 1) We need to discover what our gift is and 2) We then need to discover how to give that gift to the world.

I believe that there is no greater gift to give the world than the best version of ourselves. By discovering that best version of ourselves, we learn to love ourselves fully and are able to love others the same way.

1
WHO AM I?

'Who am I?' is an existential question we all have asked ourselves at some point in our lives.

It is said that one of the most uncomfortable questions we can be asked is, "Tell me about yourself." Do we really even know how to answer that question?

The most common responses are usually things we like to do, our hobbies, passions, interests, and even our accomplishments. But how often do we really answer, or how comfortable do we feel, answering that question in an authentic, deeper way?

I remember my first experience with this question, when it really hit me that I had no clue how to answer it.

It was my very first job. I was a young account executive at a marketing firm. On my first day, we had an orientation and all the newly hired employees gathered in a conference room. An HR executive came in, introduced herself, and welcomed everyone. She then said we would go around the room having everyone introduce themselves and a short biography about who they are.

I distinctly remember a huge wave of anxiety and panic come over me—I had no idea what I was going to say. I had introduced myself in classroom settings before, but that was super basic. It also didn't help that I was in the middle of the room and had to listen to so many other people before it was my turn.

I sat there listening to everyone tell about their elaborate backgrounds, describing other places they worked or experiences they had, my anxiety skyrocketed. This was my first job, so what was I gonna say? Was there anything to say?

THIS WAS THE FIRST TIME I ENCOUNTERED MY OWN IDENTITY CRISIS AND COMPLETE LACK OF SELF AWARENESS.

Unfortunately throughout the years it didn't get much easier. If anything, it got worse. What I mean by that is that as I continued in my career and sat in those introductory meetings, I turned it into a competition.

I would try to one-up another individual, or I would get intimidated by another person's experience that sounded way better than my own. It created an internal battle over if what I was about to say would be impressive enough to wow the group to gain the advantage.

Talk about panic and craziness over a simple question of "tell me about you!"

As my career progressed, I noticed this phenomenon even more as I got into management. When I conducted interviews, I would see and feel the discomfort people had when I asked them the same question that, ironically, had caused me so much discomfort too. I started to pay close attention to what they would say and how they squirmed in their chair, as if they had ants crawling all over them.

This was so interesting to me because I found the same response from people of all ages and walks of life. Almost everyone cringed when they were asked who they were.

Often I found their reactions amusing, but on the flip side, I totally related to them and was glad I was the one doing the questioning instead of having to respond.

When I managed a new team of employees, I noticed the same uncomfortable response when introductions were made. No matter how established they were, it was difficult for almost everyone to answer this question.

It wasn't only entry level employees that I noticed this phenomenon with—I also saw it in higher level executive meetings. I had the privilege of working for some highly reputable corporations that were industry leaders globally. Even then I saw very successful people with prestigious degrees or titles and years of impressive work experience struggle to answer this question.

DISCOVERY ACTIVITY

TAKE A MOMENT RIGHT NOW AND THINK ABOUT HOW YOU WOULD ANSWER THAT QUESTION IF I ASKED YOU, "TELL ME ABOUT YOURSELF." HOW WOULD YOU ANSWER IT?

_____

_____

_____

_____

_____

_____

_____

_____

_____

_____

_____

_____

_____

_____

_____

_____

_____

_____

_____

_____

_____

_____

_____

_____

As you reflect on how you answered it in your mind, I want you to pay close attention to what you said.

Growing up my answer was pretty standard: "Hello, my name is Jeramie and I am a basketball player. I also love to dance. I am Mexican, even though I don't look it, but I am Mexican." As I explained my ethnicity to people who had a puzzled look on their face, I felt I had to justify why I looked the way I did: "Well, Mexican people are made up of Indians, like the Aztecs and Mayans, and Spaniards, who look Anglo-Saxon. If you were to go to Mexico City you would see a lot of light complexioned people with blue eyes there." That usually was enough to start a dialogue or conversation of interest and then we would move on.

The other response I used, depending on the situation, would be to explain my Zodiac sign: PISCES. When I was about 12 years old, my mother gave me a plaque that had "Pisces" on it and some descriptive words that I would recall when asked to describe myself. Many of the descriptions I liked and agreed with, and others I wasn't really sure about, but hey—it sounded good, anyway.

As the years continued, I came up with different versions of what I would say about myself as an introduction based off what others said about themselves. I adopted parts of their introductions that I liked, but it was always so uncomfortable when I had to say it aloud.

I bring this topic up to start my book because it really is the foundational point to begin to understand the concepts of ego and our social masks.

In each scenario, I would quickly analyze who my audience was; which of my many personal bios I had put together over the years was most suited for the occasion; and what I would need to modify based off what others had said. As I went through this process over and over again, it was interesting to see how much of a chameleon I became.

> I THOUGHT OF MYSELF AS CONSTANTLY ADAPTING AND EVOLVING, BUT I NEVER REALLY CONNECTED WITH IT. INSTEAD, I FELT A GREAT DEAL OF EMPTINESS.

I came to see that this lack of knowledge about who I really was had a tremendous impact on my relationships, self-esteem, confidence, and happiness.

I began to question everyone's authenticity and wondered if there was any such thing as a unique individual. I found that most humans have an innate desire to just fit in and belong.

Others would pride themselves on being drastically different, but when they were aware I was watching they showed up very much like all the others.

This book is not only a record of my findings and the knowledge I have gained about the dual psyche we have within us, it is also my journey of how I discovered my true self.

As you go through this book, take time to reflect your on own experiences. Some of you may not fully connect with certain things, and that is okay. For those who do connect, I hope these insights lead you to the greatest gift—yourself. Not the 'you' that you might at times pretend to be, but the real, authentic 'you.'

I don't claim to know all aspects of ego, nor do I claim to be more knowledgable than anyone else. I just know that I have had a life full of experiences. Through my experiences, combined with much contemplation and personal work, I've discovered a life drastically different from the one I thought I was enslaved to.

You will likely see many of the things I talk about in others at first. We are not trained to see ourselves and be aware of how we show up. It's okay that it happens that way first. We are social beings who naturally relate our experiences and life to others as reference points. When this happens, I challenge you to dig deep and really look introspectively at your own life experiences.

2

THE BREAKING POINT

In 2008, I came to a brutal awakening—I had gotten to the point where I really had no idea who I was anymore. I was in a tornado of addiction and was constantly scrambling to cover it up. I was on the brink of an extramarital affair. I was miserable in my career and felt like nothing I did was ever going to amount to anything. I felt as if I was just doomed because my entire life felt like one big bad joke that would always allow me to scratch at a dream life, but then it would be pulled away, right out of my fingertips.

At the time, I had just turned 32 years old. I had a beautiful family, a solid career, and was an upstanding member of the community. I put a lot of effort into creating an image that, from an outside perspective, looked like I had everything figured out. However, in spite of outward appearance, I felt completely lost. I wondered,

WHO WAS I? WHY AM I EVEN HERE? WHAT PURPOSE DOES MY LIFE HAVE? DOES IT HAVE MEANING AT ALL?

I was part of a very strong and firm religion but I did not ever believe it. I went through the motions. To make my loved ones happy, I stayed dedicated to it far too long. I was in a marriage to a beautiful woman who had swept me off my feet, someone I felt I loved . . . but, looking back, I didn't even really know what love was. Somehow I found myself going down a path I swore I would never take, seeking intimate relations with another woman.

My life was passionless, it was mundane, it was monotonous, it was blah. Now don't get me wrong—my kids were the most important things in my life and I absolutely loved and adored them. I found glimpses of happiness in them, but it was not sustainable. It wasn't that they weren't enough. It was because I wasn't enough.

I felt like a failure in so many things even though I had a successful career, a nice house, multiple cars, and regular family vacations. We also traveled a lot for my kids' competitive basketball.

SO WHAT EXACTLY WAS HAPPENING TO ME? IN SPITE OF SUCCESS, WHY WAS I SO LOST, SO UNHAPPY, AND SO FERVENTLY SEEKING REFUGE FROM SELF-DISGRACE?

Then suddenly, it happened. My life exploded! I had an affair, was exposed for my addiction, and nearly lost everything that meant something in my life. I felt like I was condemned and cast out of God's eye, that I was banned from any sort of heaven.

I destroyed the ones who I loved most. I shamed my family and I shamed myself. I truly felt that feeling others describe as "the depths of hell." I was at my truest, darkest place.

I succumbed to the idea that my life's purpose must be to completely screw up my life and everyone else's who was close to me. I thought I was a monster, the ultimate loser. At least, that is what was going on inside of me and inside the walls of my own home.

However to the outside world, I was still very charismatic, had my act together, and was on the fast track to a highly successful career. I always appeared happy and positive. I was outgoing and easily met new friends and acquaintances who thought highly of me. I was able to hide behind these outside appearances, but I was experiencing serious internal turmoil. Because my world was so dramatically split, it was natural to feel the massive internal battle within me.

MY HEART WAS IN SO MUCH PAIN BECAUSE OF MY LIFE, BUT MY HEAD KEPT MAKING EXCUSES FOR WHY I WAS THIS WAY.

• "You were sexually abused at 5 years old, it's natural for you to be this way because you don't know any better and are a victim."

• "Hey, just keep everything you can a secret and it will all be okay in the end. On your death bed you can reveal if you want to and, if it's true you're going to hell, we will deal with that when that time comes."

• "It makes sense your life is a mess because of your addiction. It helps you cope and function, but everyone else doesn't know that. As long as you are good in their eyes you don't need to change."

• "Just be a success in everything else and everyone else will like you and think you are greater than you really are, that works for us."

The internal battle was fierce and constant because deep down, I knew these things weren't true, that I was more than what I was being at the time.

I knew that somehow, in the deepest corners of my heart—buried under all the shame, guilt, and hopelessness—that there was actual hope for something more.

Had there not been that small glimmer of something deep inside me, I would have just given into my life the way it was, playing into the roles I had built, the social masks I was wearing, and avoiding any real or authentic interactions.

I WOULD HAVE BECOME THE ULTIMATE HUMAN CHAMELEON AND JUST BLENDED IN TO WHATEVER CIRCUMSTANCES I NEEDED TO. HOWEVER, THAT SMALL LITTLE VOICE DEEP INSIDE TOLD ME THERE WAS MORE!

It was time to make some drastic changes in my life, but I had no idea what I was doing. All I knew at that point is that there was something more for me, that I was not meant to live this way.

Someway, somehow, the little voice inside me kept refuting every self-bashing statement I would make internally.

I started searching for some understanding and guidance through my church, through my career, through my marriage, through my family, through reading books. I looked everywhere I could to find understanding, to no avail. While people were well-meaning, somehow it ultimately lead me to greater depths of shame, greater feelings of abandonment, victimization, and hopelessness.

I was put on disciplinary action and almost kicked out of my church. I was facing a divorce and was about to lose my family.

I really was at rock bottom. At that point I was willing to do whatever it took to get back to graces with everything that mattered to me. So I entered into an addiction recovery program that would eventually be the starting point of my greatest discovery—me.

3
THE AWAKENING

The addiction recovery program I entered was highly recommended because it was part group, part individual work. It also included a program to help spouses and loved ones deal with the addiction.

I remember walking into the first meeting full of shame, disgust, and embarrassment. I distinctly remember hearing the voice in my head say, "Well, Jeramie, we will see what this bullshit is about. Just do it enough to get out of the doghouse. But you and I both know this isn't going to change anything."

I found it interesting that, when looking at couples in the program, it was easy to tell which one of them was the addict just by observing their demeanor. The addicts were beaten down, worn out, and most hung their heads low with saddened eyes of defeat. Their partners looked angry and frustrated, having a tired look that seemed to say, 'This is the last straw.'

IT WAS ONE OF THE MOST EMBARRASSING MOMENTS IN MY LIFE, BUT YET IT WAS ALSO THE MOMENT THAT I FELT LIKE THERE JUST MIGHT BE SOMETHING TO THIS FEELING I FELT DEEP IN MY SOUL, A FEELING OF HOPE AND CHANGE.

In this program we were given an assignment to write a letter to our "addict self." The counselor explained that our addict self is not necessarily our true self, but an identity or role that we play when acting out.

This concept confused me at first. Even though I had acknowledged my constant internal battle, I really had to stop to think about what he said to understand.

For so many years, the thoughts I hid deep down inside about who I really was and what type of person I was were all blended together.

I never distinguished that most of the attributes or faulty core beliefs I had about myself were tied to an alter ego, not to my true self. Needless to say, this exercise really opened my eyes to different ways of looking at things. As I worked on the assignment a whole new way of thinking emerged. As my understanding about the dynamics of human psyche grew, it started changing my life for good.

Writing my letter to my addict self was extremely difficult and painful. It was one of the hardest things I have ever had to do. It literally felt like I was writing and being brutally honest with myself for the first time in my life. I even wrote that I hated myself because some elements of myself had caused so much pain and misery not only to me, but also to others.

I STILL HAD A HARD TIME DISCONNECTING MYSELF FROM THOSE THOUGHTS. HOWEVER, IT WAS KIND OF COMFORTING TO REALIZE THAT THERE WAS AN ALTERNATIVE FACTOR TO DEFINE WHO I WAS DEEP DOWN INSIDE.

At this point in my life, I had sunk so low that I was open to all things because I was truly ready to live a different way. I was ready to explore any, and all, options for change.

I WANTED TO BE FREE FROM THE CONSTANT
INTERNAL BATTLE THAT JUST RAGED ON ALL
THE TIME. WHAT BEGAN AS A BATTLE IN-
SIDE ME SEEMED TO HAVE DEVELOPED INTO
A FULL-BLOWN WAR THAT I WAS LOSING.

As I did this activity, I reconnected with my heart. I was able to at least consider forgiving myself. I also became more aware of specific things in my life that no longer served me well. These behaviors, if anything, did more damage than good in my life.

I need to clarify that my newfound understanding of ego did not take away any of my responsibility for my actions, neither did it excuse my actions that hurt others and myself. However, it did give me clarity in understanding this duality feeling of consciousness that I had battled internally my entire life.

THIS ACTIVITY HELPED ME DISCOVER THAT
THERE WAS A MUCH DEEPER VERSION OF ME
THAT I HAD NOT GIVEN MUCH ATTENTION TO.

After finishing the addiction recovery program, I still continued to have an internal battle, but now I was more aware of it. Like most things, when our attention or focus is placed on something, it expands our understanding.

Shortly after this, a friend told me about a book he read that really helped him in his career and his mindset. I figured I would check it out. It was Deepak Chopra's "The 7 Spiritual Laws of Success."

In the chapter on 'Law of Pure Potentiality,' Chopra talks about a specific way, or reference perspective, to view things in life. As I started reading this section in the book, my whole body began to tingle and I knew that what I was reading was very important for me.

All of a sudden, there it was—the understanding I had been searching for. As Chopra elaborated on the term 'ego,' it all made sense to me. He explains,

> The ego, however, is not who you really are. The ego is your self image, it is your social mask; it is the role you are playing. Your social mask thrives on approval. It wants to control and it is sustained by power because it lives in fear.
>
> —Deepak Chopra, p.11

The word 'ego' is often used in our society to describe pride, overconfidence, or sometimes narcissistic behavior. Because I have studied psychology in school, I was familiar with the Freudian approach to ego but I didn't fully understand that. But Chopra's definition really hit home. I got stuck on the thought of what a social mask meant.

DID I HAVE A SOCIAL MASK? OR MORE THAN ONE? AND IF SO, WHAT WERE THEY?

MY MIND AND UNDERSTANDING EXPLODED AS I DISCOVERED THAT I HAD MANY MASKS, AND MANY OF THOSE MASKS WERE THE MAIN REASON FOR MY UNHAPPINESS.

I started to think about everyone around me and realized most of us walk around wearing these masks. 'I am a jock,' 'I am a mother/father,' 'I am a nerd,' 'I am a rocker,' 'I am a successful business person,' or 'I am this or that.'

All these definitions came from roles we played, or things we were called, but was that REALLY who we are?

4

FOUR CHARACTERISTICS OF EGO

The topic of ego became my obsession. I wanted to learn all I could about what ego was and how it came to be. I wanted to understand the real impact it has on our lives. I wanted to know, can we live in a different state of mind? If so, what is that state of mind? Had I ever truly experienced it?

I started to challenge what my social mask and self-image were that I had created. This gave me an opportunity to understand why I felt like I had put so much time and effort into building my life but still felt completely lost and unknown.

I started to break down definitions I found. In doing so, I discovered some common themes that finally made sense to me.

Deepak's book described some very distinct attributes of ego. Author Eckhart Tolle supported these attributes in his teachings, but he used different terminology. In his "The Power of Now," he discussed different levels of consciousness and referred to them as different "I's". He described the "surface I" as if it were ego.

My exploration lead me to understand that there are really four defining characteristics of ego. Defining and breaking down these four characteristics help us know what ego is, and how to better acknowledge and understand it.

1. SEEKING VALIDATION

We truly live in an era of ego in our society today. We seek validation in almost every facet of our lives.

Social media has completely changed the way we interact with others. We are constantly posting our lives online with the anticipation and excitement of getting views, likes, loves, emojis, and responses. We are constantly trying to prove that our lives are valuable, worthy, exciting, and always wonderful. This validation is

shaped by things that are going on both inside and outside our own self.

> OUR VALIDATION CAN BE INFLUENCED BY
> SPECIFIC SITUATIONS, CERTAIN CIRCUM-
> STANCES, PEOPLE, AND EVEN THINGS.
> —DEEPAK CHOPRA, P.10

When we seek validation, we are seeking a response
from someone or something else that gives us some sort
of approval.

DISCOVERY ACTIVITY

THINK ABOUT THAT FOR A SECOND. ON A
DAILY BASIS, HOW OFTEN DO WE SPEND
TIME THINKING ABOUT HOW ONE OF OUR AC-
TIONS WILL BE INTERPRETED OR RECEIVED
BY SOMEONE ELSE? WRITE DOWN A FEW IN-
STANCES THAT, JUST TODAY, YOU DID
SOMETHING TO GET A CERTAIN RESPONSE.

_____

_____

_____

_____

_____

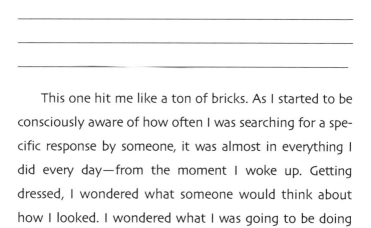

This one hit me like a ton of bricks. As I started to be consciously aware of how often I was searching for a specific response by someone, it was almost in everything I did every day—from the moment I woke up. Getting dressed, I wondered what someone would think about how I looked. I wondered what I was going to be doing at work, how my coworkers were going to respond, and what they would be thinking of me. When working out, I wondered if people would think I was in good shape or not. At this time in my life, this consumed a majority of my thoughts and I had no idea it was that way!

Ironically, one of my masks that I wore to cover up that aspect was the mask of "I don't care what other people think, I am going to do it my way." But in reality, I cared more of what others thought almost all the time.

My thoughts reflected on past memories and experiences. I remember while attending a suburb high school in Bountiful, Utah, I wore my clothes backward. It was mostly because a rap group called Kris Kross that I really liked at the time were known to wear their clothes backward, but I also did it to stand out and be different. As I transitioned away from wearing backward clothes, I sought after other trends that were unique and different from what was around me. I thought if I could stand out, then maybe I would be validated and deemed "as cool."

Basketball was also a way for me to seek validation. This brings up a great thought as well because I truly love to play basketball and is something that is a passion for me. So how could basketball, one of my passions, be a form of seeking validation? Well, it was because even though I loved to play the game, it gave me an identity that was accepted. It created another mask that I was able to hide behind, because if I was really good at basketball then others would like me. Seeking validation isn't always about obtaining approval. Sometimes seeking approval means we are also just seeking acknowledgment; and this reinforces the masks we use and carry with us to hide our true identity.

THOUGHT CHALLENGE

TAKE A MOMENT TO SIT AND THINK ABOUT YOUR THOUGHTS AND WHAT THEY ARE AS YOU GET READY FOR THE DAY.

THINK ABOUT HOW OFTEN YOU WORRY ABOUT
WHAT ANOTHER PERSON IS THINKING OF
YOU, OR HOW A CERTAIN BEHAVIOR OR AC-
TION YOU TAKE IS GOING TO BE RECEIVED
OR PERCEIVED. HOW OFTEN DO YOU GET ON
SOCIAL MEDIA AND POST SOMETHING WITH
THE INTENT OF SEEING HOW MANY PEOPLE
WILL LIKE IT?

Pay attention to the thrill of seeing a notification on your phone because you have feedback. It is important to recognize when one of our behaviors is done with an anticipation of a response, that is an ego-driven or ego-based behavior.

2. LIVING IN FEAR

Living in fear is one of the most damaging character-istic of ego and the one that binds us to ego more so than any other characteristic. Many even say that fear is the root cause of ego and so many other damaging is-sues to our psyche we have today.

THOUGHT CHALLENGE

THINK FOR A MINUTE ABOUT HOW MUCH OF
OUR DECISION MAKING PROCESSES ARE IN-
TERTWINED WITH FEAR: FEAR OF DOING

SOMETHING (OR NOT DOING SOMETHING) BECAUSE SOMEONE MIGHT THINK POORLY OF YOU; FEAR OF PURSUING YOUR DREAM BECAUSE YOU MIGHT FAIL, OR EVEN FEAR THAT YOU MIGHT SUCCEED; OR FEAR OF TALKING TO SOMEONE BECAUSE THEY MAY REJECT YOU. THE LIST CAN GO ON...

I can't count how often I have heard from my clients, family, friends, and other people that they are afraid of going after a life they want. This fear we have is not unwarranted though, and it isn't that we are just scared.

Most of us have had a tremendous amount of real life experiences that create that fear within us. I do not dismiss those experiences in any way, but we do need to realize that most of our fears are created within us and NOT because of outside circumstances.

I was abandoned in my very first experience in this lifetime. My mother was a teenage mother who decided to keep me, even though almost everyone wanted her to give me up for adoption. My biological father, or sperm donor, left before I was born. My mother married when I was almost three years old and I was adopted by my father so I don't recall much of that time. However, it was the first experience I had with being abandoned, which in turn created a fear of not being good enough or not being worthy of love and acceptance. It also created a fear that other people would abandon me at some point in my life.

To some extent, that is exactly what I experienced growing up—people abandoned me, either physically or emotionally.

IT WAS WHAT I EXPECTED BUT IT WAS ALSO WHAT I FEARED THE MOST. THIS FEAR WAS REAL AND IT DROVE OR CONTROLLED SO MANY OF MY DECISIONS.

It made me codependent in my relationships. It made me want to give my power away to other people. It created a mindset that I wasn't worthy of many things like true love and acceptance. I was always in search of something better, newer, or someone who wouldn't abandon me. I wasn't able to sit in the moment and enjoy what I was experiencing because if I did, I thought I would lose it all. This fear caused me to have an incessant need to seek validation to offset my fears.

ANY TIME FEAR IS THE DRIVING FORCE OR FACTOR IN MAKING A DECISION, SPEAKING SOMETHING INTO REALITY, OR EVEN JUST CONSUMING OUR THOUGHTS, IT IS EGO-

BASED. EGO LIKES TO CREATE PROBLEMS
BECAUSE IT LIKES TO CREATE SOLUTIONS
FOR THOSE PROBLEMS. HOWEVER, THE
PROBLEMS NEVER STOP COMING.

One of the leading indicators that ego and fear are running rampant in our minds is when we have a moment of peace and quiet—but it's not peaceful or quiet.

When we sit or lay down and our minds start to race a thousand miles per hour, thinking about almost everything that is wrong or possibly wrong in our life or world. That is when we experience the 'ego on steroids,' which over time creates so much anxiety, stress, and fear within us. It can become so powerful and devastating that it almost paralyzes us—emotionally and physically.

The unfortunate reality is that we live in a world driven mostly by fear. It is crucial for us to take inventory of our thoughts and actions to discover how many of our decisions, words, and behaviors are fear based.

When we live in fear we naturally try to find ways to hide or cover up that fear. When watching a scary movie, we put blankets over us. When we fear the monster in the closet, we leave a light on to cover up the darkness.

Fear encourages us to cover up our fears with social masks. These masks hide both the fact that we are scared and they hide what we are afraid of.

FEAR BUILDS ROUTINES AND HABITS THAT ARE VERY HARD TO BREAK SO WE ABSORB THEM AS TRUTH OF WHO WE ARE.

However our true nature is not these masks or habits we form, they are merely patterns of survival.

3. INTENSE NEED TO CONTROL

The third characteristic of ego is an intense need to control things or people. Most often we see this in areas of our lives in which we feel very insecure.

The need to control an area we don't feel safe in is a common way of dealing with our fears and our desire to feel safe. We can become obsessive in our need to control people in our lives, which can push people away.

EGO WANTS TO ALLEVIATE ANY RISK, AVOID ANY VULNERABILITY. EGO SITS IN FEAR AND DOESN'T ALLOW US TO TRULY LIVE LIFE.

Having an obsession to control every little detail of life takes away the opportunity for life to happen for us. Then we tend to live a life that just happens to us.

Discovery Activity

Take a moment to think about how many things or people you focus on controlling on a daily basis. Make a list then to write down a simple 'yes' or 'no' next to each person or thing to confirm if you actually have any control over them.

_____

_____

_____

_____

_____

_____

_____

_____

_____

_____

_____

_____

_____

_____

_____

_____

_____

_____

_____

I think in doing this activity, we will realize there is very little we really have control over.

So often this need to control circumstances, situations, or people often makes things worse in the end. It can push people away and create a distaste for life and its experiences because they don't meet our expectations of how things should be. It creates a life of routine and monotony, and doesn't allow new experiences and knowledge to come into our scope.

We can become so focused on controlling everything that we end up losing ourselves in the process. When I was in the midst of my addiction, my main focus was on control. I wanted to control what others thought of me. I wanted to control how I looked to others. I wanted to control how others treated me.

THE IRONY OF THAT WAS THAT I WAS FRANTICALLY SEARCHING TO CONTROL ALL ASPECTS OF MY LIFE, BUT THEY WERE ALL SPIRALING OUT OF CONTROL.

This pushed me deeper into my addiction. I believe this intense need to control things is one of the main reasons ego enters our psyche.

The discouraging thing about obsessing over control is that the things we truly want in our lives are pushed away because we want to control how they show up. This actually has the opposite affect and pushes those things we want away rather than inviting them in. You see this concept in theories like 'the secret' or 'the law of attraction' and so forth.

Ego is all about control. Ego wants to make us think we have control in many areas that we really don't have any control over.

4. NEED FOR POWER

Need for power is the fourth characteristic of ego. The need for power over things, situations, circumstances and even people are all the desire of an ego mindset.

THE DESIRE FOR POWER IS STRONG BECAUSE OF THE FEAR IT IS BASED ON.

However, this power we seek is temporary and is also tied to other things.

For example, power from a position or job title or career is only there as long as you hold onto the title or job. Power that comes from having money is only there as long as the money remains. The power of being physically dominant over someone is only there as long as you are bigger than the other person (or until a bigger person enters the equation).

All these aspects of power are based off temporary and external things. So, in all reality, what power do we TRULY have?

The need for power is usually connected to the need of validation. The power one person holds over another is an attempt to validate their existence by seeming superior. Other times this power may offset feelings of inferiority that lead to social masks we hide behind.

POWER CREATES A SENSE OF INEQUALITY AND JUDGEMENT BECAUSE IT DIVIDES HUMANS BASED OFF INFLUENCE AND SO-CIAL STATUS.

This aspect is one of the most present and discussed when explaining ego. So many other character defects show up because of this characteristic, such as being egotistical, narcissistic, power hungry, or chauvinistic.

Ego is much more complex than being overconfident or self-centered. Learning about these four characteristics that define ego helped me gain so much more clarity into what ego really is. It helped me understand how ego (and the different ways it influenced my behavior) had such a big impact on all my experiences.

5

WHERE DID EGO COME FROM?

Is our ego just a part of us just like our personality? Does it develop over time or is it something that we acquire somehow? Does it ever go away? Is it part of our personality? As I started to study more about ego and reflect on my own life experiences, these were the questions that arose.

I had a difficult time understanding why something so damaging would come into my psyche and was a part of me. Was it my dark side? Was it my natural or carnal man hiding inside me? Was the objective to overcome it to become more Godlike? Or was it truly something separate from me, like a split personality?

Trying to study the dynamics of human personality is daunting enough and, quite frankly, I think we still have so much we don't even know. So can we truly understand fully how ego has come about and when exactly it enters our psyche? Probably not, but here is what I have discovered through researching ego and much deep thought and self-discovery.

EGO CAME INTO OUR LIVES AS A SURVIVAL MECHANISM FOR US. IT CAME AT A TIME WHEN WE HAD A TRAUMATIC EXPERIENCE THAT CHALLENGED OUR OWN IDENTITY OF WHO WE ARE.

Most often these traumatic experiences happened in our youth, even at a very young age. Allow me to give some examples. Remember . . .

• That time you spilled a gallon of orange juice on the kitchen floor. Your mother, enraged because she had to clean it up, burst out in anger saying, "Oh you're so stupid and clumsy! Why do you do these things all the time?"

- That teacher in school who was having a rough day but took it out on you by embarrassing you in front of the class for not being very smart?

- That simple statement dad said while upset, "What is wrong with you?"

THOUGHT CHALLENGE

Think of several experiences in your own life that may have encouraged Ego to interfere with your identity.

We all have countless examples of situations in our lives, from childhood until the present, where influential people in our lives challenge who we are and our worth.

In our early stages of life, we experience pain and confusion when we feel like we are seen as broken, un-worthy, or messed up. In that state of innocence we have a difficult time understanding how we are messed up or why something is wrong with us. It is then that ego is introduced into our psyche. Ego swoops into our exis-tence as a survival mechanism, coming to help us survive those moments of existential turmoil.

EGO ENTERS OUR PSYCHE WITH A BETTER
SOLUTION THAN BEING BROKEN, LACKING,
OR WRONG IN SOME WAY. SO IT CREATES
OUR FIRST SOCIAL MASKS.

Instead of being "so stupid and clumsy" as someone called us, Ego might tell us, "You are not stupid per say, just not very coordinated and just not as smart as other people." Or when someone asks, "What is wrong with you?" Ego might say, "Well, you are just different from your siblings and other kids and being different is better than being wrong, weird, or broken." When someone says you're "dumb" or "a nuisance" in class, Ego might say, "Well, you're not as smart as some other students but they think you're funny, so instead of being smart, be the class clown."

ALL THESE MASKS THAT WE START TO AS-
SIMILATE INTO OUR IDENTITY ARE MUCH
EASIER TO ACCEPT THAN THE ORIGINAL
MESSAGES OF BEING STUPID, BROKEN,
WRONG, UNWORTHY, UNACCEPTABLE, UNLOV-
ABLE, OR JUST NOT ENOUGH.

THEREFORE EGO CAME INTO OUR LIVES AND
WAS A HERO BECAUSE IT GAVE US AN EAS-
IER WAY OF SEEING OURSELVES IN TIMES
WHERE OTHERS VIEW US DIFFERENT FROM
WHAT WE THOUGHT WE WERE.

Ego entered our psyche to help give us a different perspective. Ego was the creator of our masks.

Unfortunately, throughout the years, our ego has been in the driver seat when it comes to our own identity. It gained control of many aspects of our emotional state.

DISCOVERY ACTIVITY

THINK ABOUT THOSE MOMENTS RIGHT BEFORE YOU GO TO BED, OR RIGHT BEFORE YOU ARE ABOUT TO DO SOMETHING IMPORTANT TO YOU, OR RIGHT BEFORE YOU ARE ABOUT TO REALLY DISCOVER TRUTH ABOUT YOUR INNER NATURE. HOW DOES YOUR EGO RESPOND IN THESE INSTANCES?

TAKE A MOMENT AND WRITE DOWN A FEW OF THE THOUGHT OR EGO MESSAGES YOU GET IN THESE SITUATIONS.

_____

_____

_____

_____

_____

_____

_____

The answer is simple. Ego becomes overtly active, loud, obnoxious, and overwhelming. This creates fear, anxiety, panic, and more emotions that hold us back from truly being our self. However, the same ego that creates this panic and anxiety also loves to play the hero and create solutions for the problems it has created.

For example, at times right before you go to bed, your mind will start going 100 miles per hour about all the things you didn't get done that day, or things you need to get done tomorrow. It doesn't allow you to rest or unwind. When this occurs, we go into panic mode and tend to judge ourselves, reinforcing faulty core beliefs about ourselves. Any thoughts about getting ahead, progressing, or improving are pushed to the wayside because it is too scary and foreign. So we accept that we are stuck in the same cycle and just say, "Well, that's just how I am" or "that's the story of my life."

Because Ego wants security and does not want to venture into unknown territory, it is easier for us to just stay status quo. Les Brown says,

KNOWN HELLS ARE PREFERABLE TO STRANGE HEAVENS.

6

TELL ME ABOUT YOURSELF

One of the most uncomfortable questions we can be asked is usually the one in job interviews, first dates or encounters, or even when we start a new job or school.

I always hated being asked to tell someone else about myself, and it even made me physically uncomfortable. What could I say to seem intelligent but not expose myself? What could I say to seem funny and witty, but still sophisticated? How can I impress this person I just met that I have no idea about their background without coming across as egotistical and egocentric?

47

Most often we fall back to our 'default answers.' We share our hobbies, likes, and passions. We might share some of our accomplishments or awards we have received. We may regurgitate all the titles or feedback others have given us about ourselves, as if they were the experts on who we are. I am not claiming that those things do not have an impact, or are not connected with who we are authentically, but those things describe us at a very superficial, surface level.

During these types of conversations, Ego is on high alert. We might have thoughts like, "Oh, was that too much? Did I disclose too much information? What if they don't approve of what I told them? Maybe I didn't say enough? Maybe I should've said this or that."

WE SECOND GUESS OURSELVES BECAUSE WE ARE NOT ABLE TO TRULY ARTICULATE OUR OWN AUTHENTIC SELF.

THIS HAPPENS BECAUSE WE HAVE NEVER BEEN TAUGHT TO DESCRIBE OURSELVES, LET ALONE KNOW WHO WE TRULY ARE.

Because today's society teaches us to conform, to join groups, to take on labels or titles, that is how we have learned to describe ourselves. We are part of a sports team or a choir group. We are part of a church or political group. We are a certain title or job or project. With these titles comes judgement about them based on our own experiences and paradigms.

People who actually know themselves and can articulate it are esteemed, sought after, and referred to as authentic, but in a way that is very unique and different.

Usually these types of people are in leadership or authoritative positions. They may even be trailblazers, trendsetters, or pioneers. Whatever they are, one thing is common—they have a very firm grasp on who they are and they own it completely.

I heard a saying one time that goes like this, "It's said that knowledge is power, so as you gain more knowledge about who you are, you are gaining more self-power." I believe this statement to be true because of my own experience. As I gained knowledge of who I am, things like needing constant validation and even my urges of addictive behavior became less than before.

7

Two Voices

In my recovery program, I described to my therapist that my addiction felt like a constant battle inside me. I had felt that my entire life. The conflict was not just about one thing—it seemed to involve everything in my life.

Our Ego Voice

I remember many times my mind would race so much that I couldn't sleep, find peace, or make a sound decision. Once I decided on something, immediately an inner voice would convince me that my decision was wrong. Sometimes it would challenge me constantly as I

51

moved forward with my original choice, saying things like, "Are you SURE this is the right thing? Everyone is looking at us, thinking we are a fool," or "See, I told you it was a stupid decision and wouldn't work out." I wondered why would we would second guess ourselves, and just attributed it to lack of self esteem because that is what I was told it was.

When I was younger, I loved to sit back and observe how people behaved. Remembering those experiences, I discovered what my ego really was. I realized we have two different voices in our psyche.

MY EGO VOICE IS THE LOUD, OBNOXIOUS ONE THAT IS CONSTANTLY GOING. IT IS THE VOICE THAT TELLS ME TO WORRY ABOUT EVERY LITTLE DETAIL, TO BE CAUTIOUS ABOUT EVERY SITUATION, AND TO HOLD MYSELF BACK FROM DOING WHAT I REALLY WANT TO DO.

It's the voice that emboldens my fears and reinforces faulty core beliefs about myself. It constantly cautions me about doing something because someone else might think poorly of me or judge me. My ego voice tells me I am really not that good, or not good enough for success.

My ego voice reminds me of those areas I fall short in and tells me I need to stay in the shadows rather than step into the light. Even now it is the voice that is trying to tell me that "no one is REALLY going to read this book" because "who am I to share this information? I am no expert, I am not smart enough to write a book," and it goes on and on.

It is truly sad because we have gotten to the point where this voice has been absorbed so much that we believe it is our own internal voice of reason and logic. The great news is . . . It's not our own voice!

———————

THOUGHT CHALLENGE

TAKE A MOMENT AND SIT AND LISTEN TO THIS INTERNAL VOICE. WHAT IS IT TELLING YOU RIGHT NOW? IS IT TRYING TO JUSTIFY WHY YOU'RE READING THIS BOOK? OR IS IT TRYING TO CONVINCE YOU THAT READING THIS BOOK IS A MISTAKE AND CAN'T REALLY HELP YOU?

———————

During the recovery program we were given a task to create a trauma egg—a picturegram of the biggest personal traumas in our life. This activity creates a ton of emotion and really is challenging because as humans, we don't like to go into that little box in our mind. We stuff very traumatic experiences DEEP into the closet of our mind, hoping not to ever visit again.

It was good timing for me. When I was given this task, I was ready to live a different life which meant I was open to going back to that box. As I dove into the box, all the memories, pain, emotion, and fear flooded my mind. My ego voice went absolutely crazy and was so intense I literally felt it yelling at me.

It was interesting it started out in the role of 'victim,' meaning it was everyone else's fault why these things happened to me: My parents should've protected me and not abandoned me; that person should be in jail for what they did to me; I was only acting that way because of what I had gone through myself, and so on.

From there it went into 'attacker' mode, where my ego voice took complete responsibility and was telling me things like "You ARE a monster and something is wrong with you." It created this hostility inside me, one that wanted to go and attack everyone who had hurt me.

Once I got that out of my system, I transitioned into a 'martyr,' saying things like 'I had to go through those things so others wouldn't suffer' or 'I was the casualty because no one else would do it.'

Going through this experience with an awareness of mind, I was intrigued at the different states of being my ego voice was part of. At this time I had no idea it was my ego voice but because the program director told us to pay close attention to our emotions, I was on high alert. I later came to know that what my ego voice was doing was called the "drama triangle."

> THE DRAMA TRIANGLE IS A THEORY OF HOW WE INTERACT WITH OTHER PEOPLE WHEN WE ARE IN AN EMOTIONAL AND IRRATIONAL STATE OF BEING. FOR THE FIRST TIME IN MY LIFE, I SAW MY EGO VOICE FOR WHAT IT WAS — CHAOS.

From there I started paying much more attention to that voice on a regular basis. I wanted to really find out its affect in everyday activities, and I even questioned if it happened only when I went into trauma-land.

After we presented our trauma egg to the group and shared our experiences, it became evident that we all experienced this phenomenon to some extent or the other.

After this experience we were asked to write a letter to our "addict self," discussing how we feel about it and how we are finished being controlled by it and were going to take our lives back. This is where things really changed for me. I was so intrigued (and somewhat relieved) that I had this other alter ego or entity that caused so much pain and misery in my life.

> I HAD THIS LITTLE SHIMMER OF HOPE FLICKER INTO MY MIND THAT MAYBE, JUST MAYBE, I WASN'T AS BAD OF A PERSON THAT I ONCE THOUGHT I WAS.

I told my addict self that I was done letting my evil alter ego control me, dictate my happiness, and hurt so many people I loved. I was done being a victim. I was done attacking and fighting constantly. I was done sacrificing myself because I didn't know what else to do. As I wrote this letter of empowerment, I literally heard my ego voice laughing at me! I heard it say, "We will see. It's just a matter of time before you come crawling back to me and screw up everything again!"

> I WAS SO ANGRY HEARING IT, BUT I ALSO WAS SCARED BECAUSE PART OF ME FELT LIKE IT WAS TRUE. I WAS SO USED TO LISTENING TO THIS VOICE THAT I COULDN'T EVEN SEE THE TRUTH ABOUT WHO I REALLY WAS — AND WHO I REALLY WASN'T.

When I shared my letter with the group, once again I was astonished at how similar my experience was to others in my group.

It was one of the first times in my life I realized that we, as human beings, truly share similar experiences with some recurring themes.

I REALIZED THAT EGO IS VERY REAL AND PREVALENT IN EVERYONE'S LIFE.

Since then, I started becoming much more aware of what was going on inside my head, what my ego voice says, what it focuses on, and most of it all goes back to those four characteristics of ego.

My ego voice goes crazy when I am not validated or if I feel judged. It goes into hyperspeed when I am afraid and fear is my driving force. When I am trying to control the situation or have power over something, it is relentless, constantly telling me what I need to do to control or assert my power. This became the norm in my life so I accepted it as who I was. However, deep down inside somehow, some way, I knew that it was not me or my true voice that was speaking this way.

OUR TRUE VOICE

Once I discovered this alter ego voice that was constantly 'on,' I was curious about my own true voice — what was it?

Though I started reading self-help books and listening to motivational videos about pursuing your passions, none of these helped me understand my true voice. What did it sound like? Had I lost it? Could that be why I didn't know who I really was? That didn't make sense to me so I kept searching until I had a spiritual awakening.

I had spent a large amount of my adult life in an organized religion that my soul did not connect with. There were some things that I felt were true and, at times, I could buy into some of the core beliefs of this religion, but I never fully believed or felt this religion was for me — or any religion for that matter.

In fact, my religion had a tremendously negative impact on my addictive behavior and the way I viewed myself. Its environment was shaming, because if I did not comply with its rules than I was not worthy to receive the gifts of God. It tried to control its members by fear, hidden in doctrines like "being obedient shows the love you have," or "those who are not part of our religion cannot achieve the highest glory of God." My favorite was, "There is only one true church under heaven and ours is it." Being a part of this religion was confusing because it taught that if I wasn't 'worthy' by keeping all its rules and regulations, then I was not worthy to have God's spirit with me—the same spirit that also serves as a guide, protector, and direct connection to deity and the universe.

> SO BASED ON MY BEHAVIOR OF ME BEING ME, I WAS NOT WORTHY OF THOSE THINGS. IT FELT LIKE A CONSTANT ATTACK AND JUDGMENT ON MY SELF AND A PUBLIC SHAMING OF MY CHARACTER AND SOUL.

I was broken. I was a heathen. I was a sinner. I was unworthy. I was not allowed the grace of God. I was not able to return to His presence. Because of it, I could lose my family and all things I held dear to me, and the list can go on. These things gave so much ammunition to my ego voice that it was just overwhelming. Often the only time I could find any sort of peace was when I would give in, indulge completely, and numb myself out by giving in to my addictive behaviors. For a few minutes I would have actual peace because I didn't care at all, but afterwards I would tear myself apart and end up right where I began—if not worse.

As I started down the path to discovery in my addiction recovery program, I started to ask those questions that before had scared the hell out of me.

- Who am I really?

- Do I really come from a mean and vengeful god who only allows a few select back to His kingdom?

- Am I a devil child that is too rebellious to have joy and happiness in this lifetime?

- Do I deserve not to be truly loved and accepted? Is it my fault?

- What if what I had once believed was actually wrong?

- What if I am part of something much bigger and drastically different than what I have been taught to believe?

Well, I wanted to hit the "reset" button. I knew deep in my heart that there was more. I couldn't even explain what this feeling was, or where it came from. I just knew that there was more.

I left organized religion behind because I needed to separate from all those beliefs that I felt weighed me down. I started to explore other options and beliefs that were possibly frowned upon in the religious world.

AS I STARTED TO OPEN UP TO OTHER POS-
SIBILITIES, I STILL DIDN'T KNOW HOW
TO DISTINGUISH MY EGO VOICE FROM MY
REAL VOICE. I DIDN'T EVEN KNOW IF I
HAD A REAL VOICE.

One day as I was leaving a meeting at work, a co-worker approached me and said, "I don't mean to freak you out, but I just have to tell you that your aura is so beautiful and big." I had no clue what she was talking about so I didn't know if I should apologize or say thank you. I asked what it meant.

As she explained that we are all energetic beings who have an energy field around our physical bodies, something in my heart jumped. I started to get a tingling sensation that started from the crown of my head and went down through my shoulders into the middle of my back. The religious world teaches that this sensation is the spirit of God, or the Holy Ghost, manifesting truth. I hadn't felt it too often in my life, but I definitely felt it then. This began my journey into the realm of spirituality outside of organized religion.

I began to learn more about auras, spirit readers, energy, and being connected to something far greater than ourselves. This connection wasn't shaming. It wasn't obligatory. It just felt good. During this time I also started to learn about meditation and tried out different meditation practices until I found a few styles I really liked.

One day I was meditating, working on breathing, and quieting my mind (or my ego voice if you will), and all of a sudden I heard it. More importantly, I FELT it.

I FELT THIS SOFT SENSATION, A SOFT VOICE THAT FELT SO FULL OF LOVE. IT WAS SO COMFORTING AND FAMILIAR THAT I STARTED TO CRY.

As these emotions came over me, my entire body was flowing with energy and tingling sensations of spiritual confirmation. I finally connected to my true voice, and that voice was connected to a higher energy source. It felt like unconditional love. It was peaceful, compassionate, caring, kind, and had no other needs or desires because it just WAS.

As I sat there, I felt my true self talking and I realized it was completely different from my ego voice in almost every way.

I ALSO REALIZED WHY MY EGO VOICE WAS SO LOUD AND OBNOXIOUS! IT WAS BECAUSE IT NEEDED TO SUPERSEDE MY OWN VOICE SO THAT IT COULD BE IN CONTROL.

Now that I was aware of what my own voice felt and sounded like, I searched for it more often. I was curious to know if it had left me while I was living an egocentric lifestyle. Being aware of it allowed me to understand it hadn't left me—it was just overrun by ego.

I realized that in the still of early morning when I first awoke, and my best ideas and thoughts came to me, that was my true voice. When I meditated and could quiet my ego voice with all 'logic' and 'reason,' I could hear it again.

To my surprise, I realized that all along my true voice would usually be the one that would speak up first! I came to recognize that the first thing that popped into my head in whatever moment was the most authentic, my real voice. However, the ego voice would come in and overpower my true voice.

THAT'S WHY I FELT A CONSTANT BATTLE INSIDE ME THROUGHOUT MY LIFE—BECAUSE THERE WAS A VERY REAL AND RAGING BATTLE BETWEEN MY TRUE VOICE THAT CONNECTED TO MY HEART AND SOUL AND MY EGO VOICE THAT CONNECTED TO MY FEARS AND INSECURITIES.

I also discovered that my true voice didn't need to have any validation. It was almost comical because instruction from my true voice at times would confuse my ego voice. We see that often in life when we have genius ideas or thoughts to do something out of the norm for us—like talking to a complete stranger because of a feeling we had and that person ends up being very important and influential in our life. Logically we shouldn't have bothered that person, or it wasn't the right setting to do it. However, something within us knew it was the perfect time.

I started to learn that our true voice is related to intuition. Sayings like "trust your gut" or "trust your heart" now made more sense. I realized how often throughout my life I would get initial impressions to not go a certain way, or not do something, but I didn't listen. However, those times when I did listen to my true voice, I had amazing experiences.

8

How to Quiet Ego

Now that I understood the difference between my ego voice and my true voice, the challenge was how could I quiet my ego voice? How was I going to let go of a pattern of thinking that I had lived by for so long?

I researched as much as I could and explored all the different approaches. With so many self-help books, blogs, videos, and podcasts available, it was tough to really pinpoint a specific way to quiet the ego. It seems they all had an opinion, but was it the right solution?

Many claim that focusing on the positive and leaving negativity behind is the solution. Others teach that by merely focusing on what YOU want will drive you to the life you want. Motivational speakers talk about being able to achieve anything we want if we just focus on it.

Some of these things worked for me, but most of them didn't. Those that didn't work were usually the ones that made me feel like all I had to do was change the way I was thinking. The hard thing about this was that I have been thinking this way for over 30 years, and it was really hard to break the patterns. I usually found myself right back in my old patterns. One day a dear friend told me something profound:

TELLING US TO STOP THINKING ONE WAY AND START THINKING ANOTHER IS LIKE DRIVING YOUR CAR ON THE FREEWAY THEN SUDDENLY THROWING IT INTO REVERSE. THE KEY TO CHANGING THE WAY WE THINK OF THINGS IS TO SLOW DOWN OUR VEHICLE SO THAT WE CAN CHANGE DIRECTION.

It made sense to me. I started slowing down my thoughts and discovering new ways to do it. This helped me start changing direction. The following methods are ways I learned how to get out of an egocentric thought pattern and started to be more in tune with my true voice. I use these methods with my clients because they have proven to work well.

HOW TO QUIET EGO

STEP 1: RAISE YOUR CONSCIOUSNESS

Now that I knew my ego voice and how it was manifested, I needed to be more aware of it. By consciously focusing and being aware of it, I could learn more about it which made it lose its power over me.

I started to acknowledge when my ego was running rampant and paid attention to what my ego's messages were telling me. I started to understand with greater depth what my fears were that made my ego go crazy. I started to realize how often I was seeking validation and trying to control circumstances in my life. It was an eye opening experience to watch this unfold and see that my entire life I had been doing these things without even realizing it.

I began keeping a journal of the things I discovered like what my ego messages were and the impact it had on my life. I discovered that I was in a codependent relationship with my ex-wife and that I had constantly sought her approval and validation. I discovered that coaching basketball, which was a passion of mine, was also a way for me to seek validation based on the number of wins I got or how many great players I had created. It wasn't that those things themselves were bad, but what was concerning was the reason that I was doing them.

67

I learned why so many are labeled as 'narcissistic' and 'egotistical' because the reality is they are just living in a strong egocentric mindset, constantly seeking control and power to hide their own fears. It was really hard to realize that so much of my life was based on false pretense and false beliefs about ourselves.

> As I learned more about my ego, I came to the stark conclusion that I really didn't know who I really was because, at the end of the day, I was always striving to be what everyone else wanted me to be.

STEP 2: CHALLENGE YOUR EGO

Once I understood my ego mind frame, I started to challenge the thoughts that came up. If I got all twisted because I felt someone judged me because of the way I did something, I challenged that thought to see if it was real or if it was being fabricated by ego as a "problem."

I remember one time in particular, a player was really struggling with her game and she was trying too hard to do things she wasn't yet capable of doing. Her struggles were having a negative influence on the team. I tried to address it with her, but she wasn't interested in hearing it and she made excuses. I was concerned that her parents didn't approach me or express concern when her playing time decreased. I felt like her parents hated me and were upset because they thought I was punishing their daughter for no good reason or maybe they thought I didn't know what I was doing as a coach. So I built this huge wall of animosity and was getting angry at the parents because, after all, how dare they judge how I coach!

Finally, after a few weeks I approached them with all my built-up energy and negative emotion, getting ready to tell them they could take their daughter to find another team. Surprisingly, what happened was not at all what I had expected.

Her parents thanked me profusely for being disciplined with their daughter and holding her accountable. They were very grateful and expressed gratitude for all the time and effort I put into the team and their daughter. They supported me and my decision to decrease her playing time until she made the necessary changes and work through her struggles. This whole time I was building up a dramatic situation because I worried about not being enough or being judged as inadequate when, in all reality, they were thinking the opposite.

That was one of so many valuable lessons I learned by challenging my ego thoughts. On the flip side, not only did I learn a lot about an egocentric mindset, I also learned what a true authentic mindset looks like.

As I started to understand and challenge my ego thoughts, I became more aware of my true thoughts.

I LEARNED WHAT IT MEANT TO STOP TRY-
ING TO CONTROL THINGS AND JUST ALLOW
THEM TO BE AS THEY ARE. I LEARNED
THAT WHEN I WAS JUST BEING MYSELF I
HAD NO DESIRE OR URGE TO SEEK OUT
VALIDATION.

I was able to say 'no' more often to things that were asked of me that I didn't want to do, whereas in the past I would have said 'yes' just to get approval and acceptance. This process helped me "slow down my vehicle" that was taking me through life and let me start changing the direction of where I was headed.

9

BEHIND THE MASK

As mentioned, I wore several masks consistently in my youth. One mask was being not just an athlete, but one of the best basketball players I could be. I started playing when I was around 12 years old and I fell in love with the game instantly. I played it all the time. In winter I would shovel snow off a local court at a park just so I could practice. I spent my weekends in a gym with my basketball and ghetto-blaster radio, working on my game for hours at a time. This gave me an identity, a mask that others could see and respect.

When I played basketball, people would stop to watch so the better I got, the more validation I received. Going through middle school and even high school, everyone knew me as the basketball player—and I thought that was enough for me.

I loved to play and loved what I got back from the game. I learned so many valuable lessons about life through basketball and the battles I had. I was able to develop a good relationship with my father, who also loved basketball, and if it hadn't been for that who knows how that would've been. I made great friends along the way, traveled the country and had so many wonderful memories of playing. I bet everything on the game and the future it could provide. I received a Division 1 basketball scholarship and played against guys who had long tenure and hall of fame careers in the NBA—and I could hold my own against them.

I THOUGHT FOR SURE I WAS GOING TO PLAY BASKETBALL PROFESSIONALLY, THEN COACH AFTER, AND THAT WOULD BE THE STORY OF MY LIFE. HOWEVER, LIFE HAD OTHER PLANS FOR ME.

Another social mask I carried growing up was a bboy dancer (breakdancing). From a young age I watched my uncle dance and was in complete awe of how he moved and how cool he was. I practiced for hours in front of a mirror to learn it then started to pick up other styles of dance as the years went on. As I got to high school I would dance battle other kids and spend my weekends in the clubs when I wasn't working out on basketball. I loved this form of expression and still to this day I love to turn on music with a good beat and dance my ass off. I learned early on that girls really like guys who can dance. Perfect! It gave me more validation in a way I could control, and it even let me overpower my competitors.

I wore many other social masks for the smaller roles I would play in other people's lives, but the two I just described are examples of what a social mask looks like in our lives. Now you may be asking, why would these social masks be a bad thing? After all, they were just my passions and things I was good at. Here's why: These two masks were still limiting my full potential. Coming from an egotistic mindset, they hindered me from being completely authentic.

> I USED BASKETBALL AND DANCE TO HIDE BEHIND. I CHOSE TO ONLY SHOW THE OUTSIDE WORLD THAT PART OF ME BECAUSE IT WAS SAFE.

I could control that part of my life because of how talented and accomplished I was in it. I was able to assert power over others if needed and create an environment where I could dictate what happened. It also gave me a great deal of validation, especially when I would have local kids run up and ask for my autograph while I was at the mall, or at the clubs or school dances where a huge group of students would gather and encircle me to watch me dance. It was a great feeling to wear these masks, because on many occasions I felt like I was king.

THEN LIFE HAPPENED! The day came when I was no longer in a place in life to dance my heart away. There was also the day that basketball came to an end. I remember that time in my life so vividly. I was so angry, bitter, confused, and felt lost. I felt like a complete failure because I wasn't playing or coaching basketball professionally. Everything in my life prior was supposed to lead me into a career in basketball, and there I was . . . standing there saying, "Now what?!"

For the next ten years I tried on so many different masks. I looked toward my career for my identity mask. I looked at my family for my identity mask. I even looked to religion for a mask. All of these outside factors let me create masks, and I wore them for a time, but none fit quite like the basketball and dance boy ones fit.

THIS IS WHERE I STARTED TO REALLY
LOSE MYSELF, WHICH BEGAN A DOWNWARD
SLOPE INTO THE UNKNOWN OBLIVION OF
UNCONSCIOUS LIVING.

.

I went from a vigorous life of playing ball, dancing, and being fully engaged to a monotonous routine and accepting life as it was. It didn't take long before my passion and zest for life started to go away. I became angry and blamed my wife, family, parents, former coaches and teammates, teachers—and life in general.

I tried to excel at work, as that was the guidance I received from my dad and others, thinking that might ignite the passion again. However, it was only a temporary fix. During this low time an addiction that affected me when I was younger came back into play and really started to take hold of me and my life.

THEY SAY ADDICTION IS A REACTION TO A
DEEPER ISSUE — THAT ISSUE BEING A
LACK OF CONNECTION.

I wholeheartedly agree with this statement. I believe the ultimate lack of connection is to our true self. So as I continued to spiral into this dark world of no identity or connection to myself, I had no idea where to go.

During this point in my career I took a test from Gallup called StrengthsFinders 2.0 (now called Clifton-Strengths). At the time it was more for aptitude or career placement. I thought the test was really cool and, I have to admit, a little scary at how on point they were with my personality. According to this test, my top five strengths were Competition, Empathy, Futuristic, Individualization, and Activator. As I read through each of these descriptions, it all resonated with me and put into words things I kind of always knew about myself but couldn't quite articulate. As I read the details of my individual strengths (or talent themes as they are referred to), I could see how those things manifested themselves throughout my life.

Like most of us who have taken these types of tests I thought it was amusing, interesting, and fun but I quickly dismissed it, stuck it in a drawer somewhere, and forgot about it. In the meantime, I continued my quest to find another mask that would fit me and help give me some sort of meaning in life. I continued with work, family, and religion. I even started to coach youth basketball. I figured if I couldn't play much, I might as well coach my kids and help them enjoy the game the way I did. Although everything looked 'good' from the outside, I was still feeling that void in my life.

One day my wife was doing her client's hair, a younger lady who was talking about how she wanted to go back to school to get a Nurse Anesthetist degree. Not knowing what that entailed, my wife asked for details and thought it might be a great fit for me. As I started to research, I was intrigued by what I found because it incorporated so many things I liked. For example, a nurse anesthetist was a specialized skill set. It was in an industry that wasn't going anywhere. No one could question my performance based off someone else's performance of doing the same job. The title was cool and not well known. I only had to complete a bachelor's degree in nursing and a two year masters program and not have to deal with medical school and residency. It paid very well and consistently, which was far more appealing than a stressful, fast-paced sales job.

For the first time in a while, I was really excited about something. In fact, I was so excited about this newfound option that I asked my brother to go to lunch so I could tell him all about it. At this time my brother was a successful operations manager for a reputable company. He was stable in his career, quickly progressing, and seemed to know how to succeed and be really good at what he did.

So while we were at lunch, as I excitedly began explaining my new plan to get my ideal career so life would be blissful again, he stopped me and said, "What are you doing?" Confused, I looked at him and said, "I'm telling you exactly what I am doing, are you not listening to me?" His reply was, "I have known you my entire life and I know that you and science don't mix well—AT ALL!"

I couldn't argue that fact. However, I was older now, more mature, and was able to succeed in other areas of my life that were not even as good a fit for me as this new career. So why would I not be able to make this happen and be successful, I thought. My brother then asked me,

IF YOU HAD A CHECK COME EVERY MONTH THAT PAID ALL THE BILLS, PUT FOOD ON THE TABLE AND CLOTHES ON YOUR BACK, AND ALLOWED YOU TO NOT LAVISHLY BUT COMFORTABLY, WHAT WOULD YOU CHOOSE TO DO WITH YOUR TIME?

My initial response was, "Maybe I would go to medical school and instead of being a nurse anesthetist, I would become an anesthesiologist because they make way more money." However he said, "Stop! Think about this question and really put some time into the answer. You could do ANYTHING you wanted, what would it be?"

78

Wow, I had never thought of that before . . . if I could be anything I wanted, what would that be?

———————

Discovery Activity

TAKE A MOMENT AND THINK ABOUT HOW YOU WOULD ANSWER THE SAME QUESTION. IF YOU HAD A CHECK COMING IN EACH MONTH THAT ALLOWED YOU TO DO ANYTHING, OR BE ANYTHING, WHAT WOULD YOU CHOOSE TO DO, AND WHY?

———————

_____

_____

_____

_____

_____

_____

_____

_____

_____

_____

_____

_____

_____

_____

_____

10

The Gift

Growing up, I was never asked what I wanted to be. No one ever talked to me about what I wanted to do for a living. I was taught to work hard, and if there wasn't anything to do, then grab a broom and sweep the floors. There wasn't much discussion about the future or its opportunities.

I grew up in a very strict household. I was punished heavily for not adhering with precision to the rules. I all too well remember Mr. Belt, or whatever my father could get his hands on, even his own hands, when I fell out of alignment with their rules. I remember my mom's wooden spoons that broke often on me. I remember many days and nights being confined to my room without food or water because of my acting out.

Now, I love my parents dearly and I have a great relationship with them, but this was just the reality of it at the time. It was a generational thing. Because it was how they were raised, they thought it was the way they should raise their kids too. In his Netflix movie I AM NOT YOUR GURU, Tony Robbins told a young girl to thank her father just as much as she was blaming him for the bad things he did that hurt her. This was a shift in paradigm and an awakening for me to realize that even when bad things are done to us out of 'love,' there is still some positivity that can come from it.

We all have different pasts. Growing up, I was never taught to think about what I wanted but rather how to conform to what parents, teachers, or coaches wanted. So when my brother asked me to think about what I wanted to be in my life, it caught me off guard because I had never considered that before. It took me some time to really answer that question. Remember, at this time I was also having an identity crisis and trying to find other masks to fit me.

One afternoon, while I was sitting there sweating and breathing hard after a workout, I remembered how much I had wanted to be a college basketball coach. If I could do anything in life, I would be a college basketball coach. I could watch basketball all day long and never tire of it. At this time I was coaching my young kids in a local recreation league and I loved it. If I could figure out a way to get back to my old mask of basketball player, and change it slightly to basketball coach, and get paid for it, that would be perfect!

Excitedly, I called my brother to tell him my answer. His response was, "Now that I can believe!" then gave me another challenge. He said, "Okay, so now that you thought about an answer that makes sense, I want you to do something for me. You took your StrengthsFinder personality test, correct?" I confirmed. "Okay, pull that back out and go through that assessment again. Tell me based off that report and your natural talents why you would be a good college basketball coach."

I have to admit I was a little confused at first but I was willing to try it because I was so happy to think about being a college basketball coach. As I went through my StrengthsFinder results again, I wrote down my thoughts about why I would be a good coach based off each strength/talent. Here are notes from my journal:

COMPETITION: This is simple because in sports there is always a winner and a loser. My competitiveness has always served me well in basketball and I have won a great deal in my life. It also says that I am very strategic in how I compete and that will serve me well coaching college because it's all about strategy in creating a good program that wins.

EMPATHY: It says I care a great deal about people and I would care greatly for my players. I could connect with them and share my many experiences in my years of playing and help them learn from that. I always loved being part of a team sport and having those friendship and connections with my teammates. It would be the same for being the coach. It also says that I like to lift people's spirits and see the good in individuals and situations. This will help me make my players' college basketball experience a great one.

FUTURISTIC: This talent talks about creating a future that I can see and get people to buy into. I have seen that when I was a player by motivating my team to accomplish great things or beat teams that seemed impossible to beat. It also says I want to be in control of my own future. This has shown up a lot in my career and that is why I changed jobs so much because I didn't want others to dictate my success. As a head coach I would be in charge of it. I would be a good motivator for my players and team overall.

INDIVIDUALIZATION: This one I didn't really understand until this point in time. It talks about how I am inclined to join teams, and I have always loved being part of a team. It also says that when I am asked to determine others' special and unique traits, I am able to do so. I have always been that way as a player and a professional. As a point guard, I knew my teammates well and who liked to shoot what shots and from what locations. When someone was struggling, I knew how to get them going or help them find success. I loved making a play for one of my teammates to be successful just as much as I loved scoring on my own. It also says I get along with all kinds of people and can see what each person can do really well, even when they don't see it themselves. It says I can mix and match their unique talents together to work better and cooperate with each other rather than fight to be individual. This would help me build a team, recruit players that complimented each other, and put them in a situation all can succeed and together we win!

ACTIVATOR: The first part of this talent says, "You commonly inspire your teammates to be as enthused as you are about various jobs, opportunities, events, causes, or ideas." This is so true! This helped me as a player and will help me as a coach to motivate and inspire my team to be the best they can be and win.

I remember feeling alive again going through this process. I felt a fire burning inside me, and I got so excited I couldn't think about anything else. I finally found my calling in life I thought. I presented my results to my brother and he said it all made sense. It felt drastically different from my other plan of becoming a nurse anesthetist. He challenged me to look into what it would take to become a college coach and how feasible it would be to get into that career path.

I started to research the requirements for becoming a college head basketball coach. I reached out to my network of friends and former teammates who were coaching to ask for their guidance. I was amused that most of the people who coached tried to discourage me from pursuing it, saying how tough of an industry it was and how hard it would be—yet they were still doing it.

I was also able to connect with local college coaches and watch their practices, participate in staff meetings, and attend pre- and post-game locker room team meetings. It was a great experience and I gained new friendships from it, but it still didn't present an opportunity for me to get my foot in the door.

After spending so much time doing research, attending practices and games, and having conversations with coaches, I became very discouraged when I realized I would have to volunteer my time for an entire season just to audition for a position on the coaching staff. It was such a small and tight network of coaches that if you didn't have an 'in' with anyone, it was extremely difficult to break into the career. I didn't have anyone who would risk pulling me in, nor was I able to make a commitment financially to walk away from my successful career and lifestyle my family was accustomed to in order to backtrack to pursue my fantasy of coaching college basketball.

My ego went into high gear and the fear and faulty core beliefs about myself again came into play and kicked my ass all over the place.

Ego confirmed in so many different ways: why this was a stupid idea or why staying in my comfort zone no matter how unhappy I was still was the best option for me. I was so frustrated and no longer knew the point of trying to be happy. I fell into a deep depression.

I reached out to my father and told him about this experience. I explained how I couldn't justify doing that to my family, and all the excuses my ego came up with as to why I couldn't be a college coach. He said, "Son, you may not be able to be a college coach then if that's the case, so why don't you try to find those same types of activities, or a similar job to your current one, that you could do more of those types of activities regularly."

His advice got me thinking. It was less scary and less risky to adjust a few things in my career rather than leave it all behind to try something entirely new that offered no security. And so I left sales management and got into operations, which seemed to offer more opportunity to develop people. I saw what I loved to do as career development so I focused a lot of my energy there.

It was obviously better than the world of sales, which was all about driving business, obtaining quotas and numbers, or being very cutthroat to those who couldn't do so quickly enough.

It was at this time of great turmoil in my life that my brother told me about a career opportunity that was divinely guided. He recently went to work in operations management for eBay and said the company was a great place to work. His was a fast growing division and the largest customer service office for eBay in North America. He thought the corporate culture was amazing and there was a lot of opportunity to grow within the organization. It was very different from what I was accustomed to, as I had never worked in call centers before, but I felt good about it so I pursued it—and I was hired!

After the first year the leadership group brought in a man named Allen Fine to discuss his most recent book and speak to us on leadership. I hadn't heard of him prior, but during his speech I was mesmerized by what Allen was saying and the subjects he talked about. Like a kid in a candy store, I just couldn't get enough and felt a strong and powerful sensation inside me that I was drawn to.

I asked my colleagues about Allen Fine and who he was. They said he was a professional coach. I naively asked, "A coach for what sport and team?" They looked at me, puzzled, and said, "No, he's not a sports coach. He is a professional coach." My response was, "What the hell is a professional coach?"

In all my years, the only time I heard the term 'coach' used was in a sports setting. I had heard of Tony Robbins, Zig Ziegler, Les Brown, and so on but I only considered them motivational speakers. I had no idea there was an actual industry for professional coaching.

"This is it!" I excitedly thought. I started to research everything I could find about professional coaching. I found a program that could certify me and it wasn't overly extensive. As I went through my certification program, I felt my whole body tingle with excitement.

I KNEW THIS IS WHAT I WAS MEANT TO DO.
I FELT LIKE THE UNIVERSE AND COSMOS
MOVED TO SUPPORT ME ON THIS PATH—IT
ALL ALIGNED BEAUTIFULLY.

Remembering the lunch conversation and challenge my brother had given me years before, I again analyzed my StrengthsFinder report and compared the findings to the job of professional coaching. I felt like I was in a big puzzle that finally started to fit together.

The point of me sharing this experience with you is this: The process of trying to discover a career best suited for me, having my life fall apart, going into an addiction recovery program, becoming deeply depressed, and trying to find another mask that fit me well all lead me to the greatest thing I could have imagined.

IN THIS LONG, DIFFICULT, AND GRUELING
PROCESS, I FOUND MY GIFT—I FOUND MY
PURPOSE AND ULTIMATELY I FOUND MY
TRUE SELF!

11

THE PROCESS

It is important to understand the concepts in this chapter are just an outline of the process that worked for me and others I worked with.

I struggle with putting generalities out there because the very fiber and makeup of who I am sees everyone as their own unique individual self. However, I whole heartedly believe this outlined process will help you discover more of yourself and help find your true self.

In the introduction to this book, I described hearing Les Brown say we are vibrational beings. Those who are tuned into our frequency will hear our voice and listen to what we have to say. Les explained that the number of people who listen to us is less important than being courageous enough to speak from your heart. Those tuned into your frequency can learn and grow together.

As I explain this process, I hope it will resonate with you and the information will be as valuable to you as it is to me and others who have traveled the same path.

DISCOVERY

The first step is discovery. You need to explore more about who you are, and what characteristics make you who you are. There are many tools available to help with this, like the Myers–Briggs Type Indicator or the Color Code personality test. The ones I really like and have a strong connection to are the CliftonStrengths assessment and the Standout Report.

Use whatever makes sense to you. You can do more than one if that works best for you. I studied many different subjects in college. I joke with my kids saying I swear I tried every major there was in college. However, I ultimately settled on Psychology, which gave me an opportunity to take many different personality tests, which was fun. Using results of multiple assessments can help you see patterns about yourself. I saw these patterns for me and found that regardless of the test or who was evaluating it, specific things about me consistently showed up in my results.

The most important element in this step of the process is to just explore and discover all you can about yourself. Trust what you <u>FEEL</u> about what the results say about you.

DISCOVERY CHALLENGE

TAKE A CLIFTONSTRENGTHS ASSESSMENT TEST OR FIND A STRENGTHS COACH TO BETTER UNDERSTAND YOUR STRENGTHS AND TALENTS.

CHALLENGE & VERIFY

This next step is extremely important. It takes away doubt and changes beliefs about yourself into knowledge. There is a big difference in believing something and knowing it.

As you discover who you are, ego will keep trying to come into play to create fear or doubt any place it can. Why? Because you are leaving ego and an egocentric mindset behind and starting to connect to your own soul. Your soul has no need for ego, but fear of the unknown is always scary.

This step in the process allows you to get through the clutter. What I mean is that many people, especially loved ones like parents or siblings, give us feedback based on who they THINK we are. At times they may tell us we are a certain way, but that is because they truly wish they were that way and want us to have that quality or trait about us. At other times they may tell us we are a certain way because of the role we play in their lives or because of how they observe us interacting with others. Just because we might be perceived that way in their eyes, that does not mean that's who we truly are.

Sometimes we receive feedback about our performance and we adopt it as truth when, in reality, it is just another mask we wore to do the job. For example, my parents used to always tell me that I was a great problem solver and was very good at math. Because of that, they said I should have gone into a finance or math-related career. However, I have no interest (and really no talent) in those areas. Even though I am a problem solver, and I did well in math in school, it still wasn't what defined me. The problem with feedback from a loved one is that they sometimes tend to take a snapshot of one moment in time and use that singular experience or trait to define the whole of who we are.

Another time I was told that as a leader, I focus more on the process than on the people. Again this is far from the truth and I knew it at the time (although in my younger years when I was less aware I might have accepted and adopted that perspective of myself). By challenging all aspects of what we discover about ourselves, we can start to fine-tune the feedback and information given to us, regardless of the source. We can also challenge the way we perceive or think of ourselves, which is powerful because we are usually our own worst critics.

Let me give you an example of how to challenge and confirm these things. When I assign a client to take a CliftonStrengths assessment, we review the report together. As they read it aloud, I ask them questions that challenge if they really feel they are that way. I ask them to give me examples of when they have demonstrated that behavior.

After we do this exercise together, I give them a challenge to give their report to five people who they believe knows them very well. They are instructed not to persuade these 'reviewers' in any way other than just asking for their thoughts and opinion on if it sounds like the client in any way.

DISCOVERY ACTIVITY

NOW THAT YOU HAVE TAKEN THE CLIFTON-STRENGTHS ASSESSMENT (OR ANY OTHER PERSONALITY TEST YOU CHOOSE), FIND FIVE PEOPLE WHO YOU BELIEVE KNOW YOU WELL AND HAVE THEM GIVE YOU FEEDBACK ON HOW IT RELATES TO YOU.

_____

_____

_____

_____

_____

_____

_____

_____

_____

_____

_____

_____

_____

_____

_____

_____

_____

_____

I ask them to also make a self-awareness journal where they pick one trait they aren't quite sure about, and for a week or two they observe how this trait manifests itself.

———————

DISCOVERY ACTIVITY

BEGIN A SELF-AWARENESS JOURNAL BY TAK-ING ONE TRAIT AND OBSERVING HOW IT MANIFESTS ITSELF IN YOUR LIFE FOR TWO WEEKS. ALSO WRITE DOWN THE OUTCOME OF THAT TRAIT IN ACTION.

———————

_____

_____

_____

_____

_____

_____

_____

_____

_____

_____

_____

_____

_____

After consciously challenging the traits, behaviors, and elements that make up who we are, we can have a much more clear understanding of what is true and correct about ourselves. Our own awareness and consciousness of who we really are and how we show up becomes evident. In fact, if you see those behaviors or traits happen over and over again on a consistent basis and you have a report that helps you articulate those specifics about you, these beliefs transition into knowledge.

When I went through the process myself, this step helped me tremendously. I had so many faulty core beliefs of myself—beliefs that I wasn't worthy because I'd been abandoned so much; beliefs that I was narcissistic or selfish because of how my addiction was manifested; beliefs that I had no value; or beliefs that I was manipulative and couldn't be trusted.

> IT'S IMPORTANT TO UNDERSTAND THAT WE
> NEED TO CHALLENGE <u>ALL</u> OF THE BELIEFS
> WE HAVE OF OURSELVES.

Previously I used an analogy of driving a car to discuss how, when we are used to thinking one way about ourselves and all of a sudden try to reverse those negative thoughts into positive ones, it's like throwing a car into reverse on the freeway (see page 68).

Well that doesn't work. We need to slow the car down before we make directional changes. This process to challenge and verify is one way to slow down our thoughts about who we really are. What I mean by this is that when we are told to think the opposite and positive thought contrary to our negative thought that we are going to be in a better place. NO, not true! If I think about myself as being selfish then the opposite of that thought is that I am selfless and have to completely give everything of myself to others. Well, this creates a life of being taken advantage of and self-sacrifice so much that we lose ourselves completely.

As we challenge thoughts or characteristics about who we are, maybe we learn we can be selfish in specific ways that help us keep balance in our lives, and in other ways we can become more selfless. This is our level setting step. In other words, we are discovering where we are right now. We are getting to the core of what lies behind the masks we used and carried throughout our lives. It solidifies things we think about ourselves with evidence confirming we are that way and clears the space from those things we think we are, but are not.

LET GO OF JUDGMENT

Letting go of judgment is the hardest part of the process.

ONE THING YOU NEED TO UNDERSTAND IS
THAT THESE REAL AND AUTHENTIC TRAITS
(OF WHO YOU ARE) ARE JUST TRAITS. THEY
ARE NOT GOOD OR BAD, THEY JUST ARE.

We must understand how these traits can benefit or hurt us and others. For instance, my top strength in my StrengthsFinders report is competition. Now anyone who really knows me knows I am VERY competitive, and I have been since my youth. Growing up, this trait served me very well when it came to winning and being successful at basketball. It pushed me to be better and work harder, and it gave me opportunities in my life that I may not have had otherwise. This is a good trait then, right?

Well, years later I started to coach young girls basketball. As a player I was a winner. I was intense and gave my all-out on the court every time. I hated losing. If that worked for me as a player, then shouldn't it work for me as a coach?

I tried to use that mindset going into coaching. I knew my strength was competition so I was going to help these girls be winners like I was. We were going to win. I was so intense my first year coaching that people thought I was crazy. I never personally attacked the girls in any way, nor did I degrade them. However, I did challenge them to be their best, but a deep-voiced man standing

6'2" and 280 lbs scared them at times. I challenged officials who were slighting us and sometimes I even got kicked out of the games.

Now we won a lot that first year. We made it to every championship game of every league and every tournament we played in. We even won a regional tournament in Las Vegas by the end of summer. At the end of that first season I took some time off and evaluated that first year. I pulled out my StrengthsFinder report again and reviewed it in case I might be missing something. I was so proud of the girls and the success we had but I wasn't very proud of myself. I reflected a lot on the times I was too intense.

As I went through my results again, as I had so often before, I saw something I hadn't noticed before. On my Competition strength it says, "A second or third place finish can send you into an emotional tailspin." A-HA! No wonder I hated losing and it wasn't good enough to finish second or third. An emotional tailspin was exactly what I experienced that year if we lost.

I discovered another nugget of key information as well. The next sentence says, "Your ability to pull out of it depends on your other talents." I had never paid much attention to that part of the description before because I was more focused on that being a "good" positive strength. I had to go back and process that information and now challenge it.

It was the first time I consciously recognized that I am competitive by nature, and that was who I am. However my competitive side can have a positive affect by allowing me to win and accomplish things, but it can also have a negative impact on me if left unbalanced or unchecked.

We cannot judge ourselves and who we are because we are exactly as we should be. We are here on this planet to learn and experience things to give us more knowledge. One size does not fit all. One way of being is not the answer.

WE MUST UNDERSTAND WHO WE ARE—AND WHO WE ARE NOT—AND LEARN TO BE COMPLETELY OKAY WITH IT.

CREATE INTENTION

After we have discovered who we are then proven and accepted who we are, the last step is to create intention behind it. This magnificent process and experience of true self discovery has lead us into a position to pursue a full life and know what gifts we can offer the world.

When I discovered that I was not analytical or good with scientific equations and biology, I was able to leave behind my plan to become a nurse anesthetist to eventually find my true passion. Had I made a career out of being a nurse anesthetist, I would have been left wanting or feeling empty.

> WHEN I DISCOVERED WHAT WAS UNDER MY
> MASKS, I WAS ABLE TO SEE CLEARLY WHO
> I WAS AND WHAT I HAD TO OFFER THIS
> WORLD. I FOUND A PATHWAY THAT FIT MY
> TRUE SELF AND THE UNIVERSE SUPPORTED
> ME WALKING THAT PATH BECAUSE IT
> ALIGNED WITH MY PURPOSE AND SOUL.

As I continued to create intention of what kind of life I wanted to live, I became more aware of how my traits could affect others. I knew when I could manipulate and when I could motivate, and what the difference was. Then from there I made a conscious choice to motivate. I learned when I needed to be competitive and when I needed to more empathetic with others and made the conscious choice to do so at the right time.

> I LEARNED THAT NO MATTER WHAT I DID,
> I WASN'T GOING TO BE ABLE TO PLEASE
> EVERYONE ALL THE TIME AND THAT WAS OK—
> AS LONG AS I WAS BEING AUTHENTIC AND
> TRUE TO MYSELF!

12

INTO THE MIRROR

Now that you have the process in which to discover what really lies behind the social masks you have been carrying all these years, it's time to accept the magnificence that lies within you.

When I spoke with a dear friend and fellow addict about our experience in the addiction recovery program, he semi-seriously joked, "How long do you think we have until we are back here?" I remember thinking—or rather hoping—that it would be a very long time, but something inside of me said it may not be. I didn't know how to answer him at that moment. As I pondered that thought for months afterward, I hated the thought of returning and asked myself WHY?

WHY IN MY RECOVERY PROGRAM DID I HAVE TO SAY <u>I AM</u> AN ADDICT? WHY IN TWELVE STEPS DID I HAVE TO IDENTIFY MYSELF AS 'A RECOVERING ADDICT?'

This led to more questions . . . Why was this addiction like a sickness that didn't have a cure? Why was I born into this world as 'nothing more than an addict?'

In the following years I started to learn more about myself. I learned I am not one who likes titles or being put into boxes. I started to challenge that idea of "being an addict." As I learned more about my true nature, I challenged those things and beliefs and came to KNOW more about who I really was. The title of 'addict' (and all the things that came with it from my past) became less and less real.

Understanding my past and the abuse I endured, the trauma I experienced, and the abandonment and faulty beliefs about my value all dissipated into what seemed another lifetime ago.

GROWING UP, I HATED TO LOOK IN THE MIRROR. I WAS ASHAMED OF WHAT I SAW AND WHAT IT REPRESENTED. UNDER THOSE

MASKS I WORE, I COULD STILL SEE MY
TRUE EYES AND KNEW I WAS HIDING SOME-
THING THAT MUST NOT HAVE BEEN WORTH
ENOUGH TO SHOW.

I was petrified to remove my masks to see what really lied underneath. The quicker I could get ready and leave the mirror, the better. But I was never fast enough to get rid of the uneasiness I felt when looking at myself in a mirror. It was like this throughout my life . . . until one day something changed.

Years after I left the addiction recovery program, worked this process and came to learn what really lied behind the masks, I looked into the mirror and saw something—something familiar, something genuine, something real.

THAT DAY I SAW MY TRUE SELF IN THE
MIRROR FOR THE FIRST TIME IN MY LIFE.
AFTER 37 YEARS, I FINALLY SAW WHAT
WAS BEHIND THE MASKS!

I started to cry! My tears were filled with sorrow and pain from the past. They were not shameful, but tears of compassion for what I had gone through. They were tears of joy for where I was at and the journey I took and endured to get where I was now. They were tears of humility and strength tied together, knowing the battles I had been through—the ones I lost and the ones I won. They were tears of hope—hope for a better life, hope for myself, and hope that others could find their own true self. Most important, they were tears of love.

I saw my light and soul for the first time out in the open and lovingly accepted that person I saw right in front of me. I was no longer the monster I thought I was before. I was no longer the unworthy of love and abandoned child. I was no longer the addict. I was just me . . . for good or for bad, I was me—and I was 100% good with that. So I send this challenge out to all:

TAKE OFF THE MASKS AND LEARN THE BRILLIANCE THAT MAKES YOU, YOU.

I know it can be very scary, challenging, and at times it might even seem impossible. However, I have experienced it for myself and have had the privilege of seeing others go through the process for themselves.

I PROMISE you, there is no greater work than this in your life—the work of coming to know, and love, the real you.

To be yourself in a world that is constantly trying to make you something else is the greatest accomplishment.

—Ralph Waldo Emerson

Suggested Resources

SELF-ASSESSMENTS

Myers-Briggs

Color Code

High Five

CliftonStrengths

Standout Report

ADDITIONAL READING

"The Power of Now" by Eckhart Tolle

"The 7 Spiritual Laws of Success" by Deepak Chopra

"The Gifts of Imperfection" by Brene Brown

"The Alchemist" by Paulo Coelho

About the Author

Growing up I had aspirations to have a career playing basketball. I had amazing experiences traveling the country, playing against guys who would later become NBA Hall of Fame candidates. I was a high school star and earned a full-ride scholarship. My life was on track right?! Well not necessarily . . .

Life has a funny way of turning things upside down. As my basketball career came to an end, I was left wondering 'what the hell am I going to do now?' Like so many, I just worked doing anything I could—constantly chasing money, status, titles, and trying to keep up with the Jones's.

At some point, I came to a rude awakening that I really had no idea who I was or what I was even good at. I tried to study every type of degree looking for answers. I worked in many industries, jumping from job to job trying to figure it out. To my dismay I still felt clueless and had no answers.

Taking the Gallup Strengths Finders assessment was a pivotal moment that launched me down a path to discover myself. I changed direction in my career and ultimately discovered my true passion—coaching! All types of coaching—life, career, strengths, addiction recovery, corporate, team coaching and also basketball!

Through my coach training, I obtained three certifications for different modalities which helps me be the best coach I can be. My expertise is helping others discover their true self. Through a process I created, I help others find their natural talents and strengths and fully understand how their strengths impact others, create value, and build a blueprint to create even greater focus for their life.

I also work with teams and team dynamics. With most of my career spent in a team-oriented environment combined with my experience playing and coaching basketball helped me learn how to assess team strengths, weaknesses, and how to help teams transition to great performance. I also work with leadership to understand how to manage a high performing team, using talents and strengths of their team members. My process has lead teams to increased engagement, higher productivity, and greater profitability.

These things are my purpose, my value add to the world. My heart yearns each day to help others turn the light on to discover their own brilliance and magnificence that lies within.

Discovering this myself is one of the greatest things I've experienced in my life. Being a coach is not a title or a job to me, it truly is my way of life.

To know more about my work, my podcast, and how to contact me for coaching, speaking, or other needs, please visit my website

www.selfalchemists.biz

Made in the USA
San Bernardino, CA
03 August 2020